Self-portrait as a diviner, failing

Michelle Penn

in memory of my parents

and

for Jonathan

Self-portrait as a diviner, failing

First published in Great Britain in 2018
by Paper Swans Press

Poems copyright © Michelle Penn 2018
Selection copyright © Paper Swans Press 2018

All rights reserved

ISBN 978-1-9998196-6-8

Printed in Great Britain by Jasprint

paperswans.co.uk

Contents

Self-portrait as a diviner, failing   5

Family Portrait   9

Alterations   10

The son returns from abroad   11

My mother considers altitude   12

Floating   13

Family Portrait   17

Dazed   18

initiations   19

exodus of the dolls   21

every evening for months   22

Private Apartheid   23

the weight of blood   24

learning to hear   25

Social   27

one of the tribe   28

Family Portrait   33

Self-portrait as *muti*   34

Self-portrait as a diviner, failing

    Face and arms bruised by the sun, bare feet
bleeding clay, I'm calling,
        I have the questions —

    calling,
        Come to me —

    The amulets, the potion pots weight
my neck. I'm clutching
        at sacred barks,

    calling,
        Send me a vision —

    calling,
        Speak —

Words
    are only dried wings. The spirits have turned away,
            my bitter tribe
                divided
    back to pale names, villages
        too far cornered for compromise.

My lips crack, split

    and still I'm calling, *Please —*

        I know the shuddering and the spells.
        Bring me the dreams.
        Guide me through this fitful pass, this
                misunderstanding —

1.
'Lithuania on the Veld'
(South Africa, 1931-1969)

Family Portrait
Atlantic Ocean, 1931

Chana watched the ship's bow tear
    the ocean's seams. Her son,
        my father, still in swaddling; her husband
            elsewhere.
                    He would find them,
                        when he could.

Europe was a pinhole, closing — Rokiskis to Libau
to London and out
before another too-late struck them.

She was no naïve tailor's wife. She knew
        hunger's suck and how steel
    could gut skin, had seen those she loved
            slashed down like so many rats.
        She knew the Quota Act wasn't exactly

a welcome mat. Yet here she was, village girl
on a mailboat, imagining Africa

        in Yiddish, holding out one pale winter hand
           toward the Cape of Good Hope.

Alterations
Johannesburg, 1948

His past a hidden seam, days a train of cigarettes
and stitches — trouser cuffs, brace buttons,
wide-peak lapels. Tobacco muting the edges

of memory: sixteen and hoisting a rifle
in a conscript's fist, the Tsar's metal forever
threaded through his flesh. Outside, the world teeters

from another war to end all wars. Chickens squawk
in the yard and new laws of apart-
ness cinch their grip. Yet he holds to his tasks

smoke after smoke, the sewing machine's *rat ta tat tat*.

The son returns from abroad
Johannesburg, 1959

So this was home. From the Queen's English to *Where does it hurt*
in Zulu. Back to the game of homelands, to parents
who sewed a thousand suits to school a surgeon, sisters nesting

pleased as grebes. Days spent in Soweto's mouth: patients
a fountain of metal — machete to the chest, switchblade
to the thigh, ears spear-torn and split. Tribes teaching him

new sides of spite, his needle granting no reprieve.
But what else was there? Another Jew-boy bounce, a foreigner
everywhere — *Kubuhlungu kuphi?*

In how many lands would he learn to ask?

My mother considers altitude
Johannesburg, 1969

She was used to living at altitude, correcting for the rise above the sea, adding more liquid to keep cakes moist. Moist as a kiss. She kissed their cheeks, his two sisters, finally faces instead of names — five years after the wedding. Obligatory *braai* in the garden, beef on the fire, ears of corn smoking. The meat was tough. The eldest sister wielded her keys: telephone locked, pantry barred. The servants would steal everything. Both sisters eyeing her, their smiles dry. The American who kept their brother far, some princess who never saw sacrifice. Decades later, those moments still prick. The meat always tough, and the cakes. The cakes.

Floating
Johannesburg, 1969

An inner tube and inflatable bracelets cradle
the American child. A strange part of town, this —
skin the right colour but the god all wrong;

streets of Lithuanian tailors, the clans they raised, carefully
keeping close to their own. Dandled by waves, the child
sees high heels on concrete, a straight skirt

skimming knees. Not the black housekeeper who babysat.
Perhaps the mother. One of the aunts or the grandmother,
who will fade to mere names. The memory remains forever

truncated: legs, water, weightlessness.

2.
Apartheid wasn't only an Afrikaner word
(USA, 1973-1982)

Family Portrait

She was a sorceress, all angles. Her silhouette
cut the celadon sky, she knelt
     beside a child —

          bead-laden, belly like a gourd —

          extended spindly fingers toward him: her son

             or her prey?

That canvas
was the work of a witch doctor. I'd been told
     and I believed it —

          the way her wrist wraggled

inside her bracelets
     her hand reaching

             gathering ancestors
             to cast her spells, spirits
             of misfortune — madness, even.

I loved her. But I worried
about the boy,
     at the mercy of so many

          powers he couldn't understand —

Dazed

'... after a 1974 Supreme Court ruling to desegregate Denver schools, the buses rolled, carrying as many as a quarter of the city's students to schools far from their neighborhoods...'

—*The New York Times*

The fear was that we would sleep too long,
sleepwalk too far. Embark
upon that simple excursion to where minds
open their first malignant buds.
A noble idea, to wake us before

we could sleep, before the world could hiss
in our ears that dreadful
word: skin.
Only they were too late.

We arrived with eyes yawning, swallowed
the glare without a blink. White chalk
on black board, there could be nothing
more obvious. All of us

together, roaming blindly, bumping
into walls, tumbling from chairs, dragging
our tongues along white-scrawled sums,
chewing the dark skin of the film
sliding along the projector's eye –

The fear was that we would sleep too long.
But they never taught us
what it meant to be awake.

initiations

1.

girl admiring the page (deliciously afraid)

marked
    smeared with clay: deep faces
        budding muscles
            whitening dry

    shades
of the boys
whose bodies
they have vacated —

forelock, foreskin, for a time
    marked, apart

        they have suffered the cut
        and stand, solemn
            waiting —

        first, the word: *this is a man*

        the word: *this is how a man behaves*

            he never brings his father shame

the elders, the lessons
then they race
naked shades of clay

    to the river

    to wash off white and stand
        as men

            once again definite

2.

girl recalling the page (betrayed)

the shades trail her days
   marked, apart —

      deep faces
      whitening dry
         the cut, childhood
         buried with the skin
            that held it

      and they show no emotion, none —

they trail her days
   the bus, the bracing
   stretch to terrain
     where she is too

         definite, pallid
         as talc

           her first cut: *honkey*

           the next: *bitch*

   and his word, solemn:

       show no fear, no pain
         do not shame
       yourself, do not shame

            your father —

The poem evokes elements of an initiation ritual practiced by the Xhosa, Thembu, Mfengu and Bomvana peoples. It also alludes to court-ordered bussing in order to desegregate schools in seve American cities.

exodus of the dolls

the doll stared head of black beads hard-colour dress
tight around a metal cone   souvenir from the parade
of relatives escaping a land strangling itself staying a
night or a week on their way to someplace else   they
brought comic books biltong and the mysterious gift
of underwear as though the american cousins were
running naked beneath their levis they brought dolls
i preferred my barbies   they had their own airplane
and an expandable penthouse   still the dolls kept
coming a flat felt blonde sporting yarn braids and a
blue dress a grinning brown baby in a woolen wrap
a pair of feathered warriors clutching spears   my
parents only got names   who had left   who was
leaving who was thinking of leaving suitcases and
suitcases stuffed with dolls

every evening for months

two aunts sit knitting needles steady click click click click click click hands lift and loop the ball of wool twists on the floor twitching to the clicks   two aunts sitting on the striped couch never looking at their hands never needing to not even to start a new row their fingers know knit and purl   they plait fat cables across a piece of sleeve needles ticking off the seconds in the home of family they barely know nothing to their names but their names everything left in apartheid's machine   click click click yet they seem so sedate eyes fixed on masterpiece theatre monday night football the weather as they churn out sweaters and blankets my mother begins to hate click click click click click click click click through news wars mass suicides protests death   all the world is discord and they never drop a stitch

Private Apartheid

In the dining room, eleven sets of elbows collide *Please pass the salt. And at school today?* This house the mother's turf, even with her husband's sisters entrenched in the guest room, the niece squatting in the daughter's bed, four extra sons invading the basement. Everyone so polite, so careful with the good china (only her wedding service serves so many). Every day after work, the mother separates whites from darks, measures detergent. Prepares another meal. *Just until they get back on their feet.* Every evening, she sits closest to the kitchen, where something is always boiling —

the weight of blood

the grandparents echo their photos
just more crumpled

jet-lagged, standing in the entryway
for the introductions.

he is a cigarette thread, his face
the dimmer version of your father's

man as parenthetical phrase, dissolving
into the walls. her accent sketches

a ramshackle *shtetl*, crooked alleyways
detouring vowels into unfamiliar gutters

and she smells of heaviness, of a history
the girl has only heard in whispers, foreign

words: *pogrom* could be *programme*,
pilgrim, pompom. the woman's

flaccid arms engulf, words suddenly clear,
in all their looping madness, *you are*

my blood.

learning to hear

in the bathroom
after school
a fifteen year-old
presses ice
to her earlobe
purifies the needle
inside a butane flame
pushes the point, black
with heat, through
frozen flesh

the mother: *just what*
           you need
  — another
    hole in your head

the father: *Zulus believe*
    ear-piercing opens you
        to wisdom
  — rub
    alcohol on that

and the words
of her days
sound louder than ever
honkey bitch
I'll kick
your ass
I refuse
your family can
rot in hell
and the ear

becomes infected
crusted
with yellow pus

thirty years on
the hole is gone
only the slightest scar
marking the rite and all she
can never un-hear

The father refers to the Zulu rite, *ghumbuza*, in which a child's ears are pierced to bring forth the adult, who is able to hear and understand.

Social

It was their music, half-talk, half-song, reverberating off cracked plaster, the steady bass marking the minutes until we rushed for the bus. They danced in rhythmic jerks, seemed to know the words and what to do with their bodies. Across the room, my friends and I stood in clots. We only swayed to slow songs at parties after Truth or Dare.

But if I crossed that cafeteria, tried to move to their beat?

I didn't. I stood and looked. The floor vibrated. Midway, the music changed to the wailing metal our boys liked and I found myself lurching to a different bass, insistent as a propeller, revving up, going nowhere.

one of the tribe

      a thimble
                  of blood   *hold it*
         it's nothing   just a thimble
      and blood
         is mostly water

      two minutes:
            my outstretched arm
supports it   easily
     such a small thing   a thimbleful

     ten minutes:
   a sliding ache sours   blood weighs
more than bone   is thicker   than memory
    and whose rite   is this
      whose
        obligation?

     twenty minutes:
  a hard pulse   churning
      my arm   stutters
    searing   flaring
      then numb

    thirty minutes? sixty?   i
      no longer know   but *hold it, hold it*

my arm gives way
        thimble clattering   blood spilling
            my hand twitching
    fighting   to erase
                           failure
empty palm
     frenzied
                   against
          the lightness
            of air

3.
Searching for rituals
(France/United Kingdom, 1999-2016)

Family Portrait
Paris, 1999

Then I remembered her —
    silhouette carving
               the celadon sky, limbs
   slender as aloe. She knelt
beside the child

       lithe fingers reaching —
               — suspended —

       — my father —
       — suspended —
in a sleep without dream

If you speak, he might hear.

I gathered passport, ticket
      the black dress
     and summoned her
   from the wall of my parents' house

      the diviner, chosen for her visions
        her dreams without sleep

        to her the spirits whispered their will —
     She extended

one hand toward the boy,
       bangles jangling, a dance,
   an incantation:
   It will never be too late —

Self-portrait as *muti*

        first, strip away the smile
        fling it to the floor with the clothes

        make an incision down the centre of the chest
        and peel back the skin
                roll it like a surgeon's glove
            layer over layer until
                it slides off the hands
                        (your gentlest touch)

            until you step out of it
                    (the quietest tread)

            until you flip it, like hair
            off the crown of your head
                        (nodding nodding in silence)

toss all of it at the stag bash in one corner – *Here, boys! Vavoom!*

        dislodge the lacy yellow fat
        plumping your belly breasts thighs
                    (a lady always —)

aim it at the front-row girls — *Here's a boa, my lovelies!*

            And here! the cartilage of your nose
                    (are you a —)

            Here! the hard swirl of an ear
                  (smile baby I know you hear m

Here! the larynx
(if you can't say something nice —)

Take it!
Take the lot!

claw open your skull, unravel tendrils of brain
(they're all like that — what you looking at,
honkey girl — whose side are you on —)

Here! Whoever wants it!

flaunt everything: your bones muscles organs blood
revel in the taboo

then give, offer yourself
cure the world's indecencies

Muti refers to ingredients of traditional South African medicine, including plants, minerals and animal organs.

Michelle Penn grew up in the US and lived in France for seven years. She has a BA in Psychology from the University of Michigan, along with MAs in French and Comparative Literature from the Sorbonne. For many years, she wrote and produced multimedia guides for museums around the world. She recently completed a book-length poem and is working on a novel. A dual US/UK national, she lives in London.

Acknowledgements

I'd like to thank the editors of the publications where some of these poems first appeared:

'Self-portrait as a diviner, failing' was published in *Spillway* (USA). 'Family Portrait' (page 17) was first published as 'Family Portrait I' in *Prodding the Pelt* (Salmon Poetry, 2017). An earlier version of 'Family Portrait' (page 9) was originally published as 'Family Portrait II' in *The Wolf*.

Warm thanks to the following people for early feedback on some of these poems: Jill Abram, James Byrne, Graham Harthill, Andrew McMillan, Ruth O'Callaghan, Kathleen M. Quinlan, Fiona Sampson, Kim Schoen, and Susan Terris.

A huge thank you to Abegail Morley and, of course, to Sarah Miles.

Finally, my love to my brother, Jonathan, and to all of my friends. You lift me higher than you know.